Celebrations

journal belongs to...

© 2016 Ranch House Press
All rights reserved. Printed in the United States of America.

www.annettebridges.com

ISBN: 978-1-946371-14-0

Journal Prompts
Celebrations

Celebrations then or now. Journal your traditions of yore or about new ones you want to begin.

1. What are your family's favorite baked goods during the season and who is most likely to bake them?
2. Do your Christmas traditions include throwing or attending an annual Christmas party? What are your favorite activities? Carols? Games? Drinks and desserts?
3. Were you part of a church Christmas pageant or ballet as a child? Are you still?
4. Christmas Eve. Do you have a traditional meal? Do you attend a church service? Is it a midnight service? Does family gather? Do you open any presents on Christmas Eve?
5. Christmas Day. What's for breakfast on Christmas day? Do you open presents on this day? Do you visit others or have family come in for a meal? What do you eat on Christmas day?
6. Take the last line of your favorite Christmas carol and use it as the first line of a poem.
7. Imagine yourself at age 10. Write a letter to the 10-year old you explaining what celebrating Christmas means to you.
8. Describe in detail your favorite Christmas decoration.
9. Tell about a Christmas gift that you were most excited about giving.
10. Share some of your family's Christmas traditions.
11. Describe the Christmas tree at your house.
12. Besides home, where would be the perfect place to celebrate Christmas?
13. Tell about a memorable encounter with Santa.
14. Plan and describe the perfect Christmas meal.
15. How do the sights and sounds of this holiday season affect your mood?
16. Pick one of your favorite holiday songs and illustrate it.
17. Create a snowflake. Doodle them, paint them, make them out of popsicle sticks, use glitter nail polish, the possibilities are endless.
18. Build a snowman. You don't have to go out into the cold to build a snowman. You can always paint, draw or doodle one.
19. Create a journal page inspired by the word "presence" and the people who have been a gift to you in your life.
20. Paint or create a winter scene of evergreen trees or decorate a Christmas tree. There are so many ideas for making trees such as out of twine, ripped out book pages, buttons and more.
21. What are your wishes and wants for the holiday season this year?
22. Write about your own ghosts of Christmas past, present and future.
23. Do the holidays make you feel stressed or sad? Create a list of ways to help lift your spirits during the winter months.
24. Explore how other countries celebrate the holidays and create a page of ideas that interest you the most.
25. Design your own ugly Christmas sweater.
26. Favorite Christmas as a child….
27. Who I'm missing this Christmas…
28. I can't wait to bake….
29. I'm dreaming of ….
30. I am most thankful that …
31. If you could give yourself a gift, what would it be?

color your world

ABOUT the CREATOR

Annette Bridges is an author, publisher and women's retreat host on a mission to help every woman realize her story is extraordinary, valuable and noteworthy.

She has published the *Color Your World Journal Series* and formed a journal club to provide community, support and tools for women to record their ideas, feelings, experiences, memories and all the important details of their lives.

Before writing books and publishing journals and coloring books, this former public school and homeschool educator spent a decade writing hundreds of helpful, instructive, and light-hearted columns published by Texas newspapers, parenting magazines, websites and bloggers.

Annette lives on a Texas cattle ranch with her husband John, dachshund Lady and lots of cows. She can drive a tractor but only if wearing a fresh coat of lipstick and it's not her pedicure day!

You can learn more about Annette's books and products, blogs and videos as well as her women's retreats and other events at www.annettebridges.com.

Look for her on social media, too!

MESSAGE from the PUBLISHER

The **Color Your World Journal Series** is a pathway to self-discovery. It's where you write notes to yourself. Be your own cheerleader. Give yourself encouragement. Tell yourself what you're grateful for. Celebrate you!

There are countless reasons to keep a journal including collecting favorite recipes, listing goals and celebrating every experience and every one that's near and dear to you. A journal provides a home for the memories and lessons learned that you never want to forget.

Why a niche journal?

If you're anything like me, you have a journal (or even two or three journals) where you write anything and everything about anything and everything. My challenge comes when trying to find something I've written. I flip and flip through the pages of my two, three or four journals trying to find whatever it is. I never remember which journal I wrote down my whatever's!!

The solution? A niche journal! A journal that has a specific focus and theme! A journal where you can record your ideas, inspirations and things you want to remember in the appropriate journal.

Why big unlined paper?

Because big unlined paper is needed to record big ideas, dreams and memories! You need room to grow, stretch and expand. You need space to think beyond the confines of what you've always done, to pursue new dreams, discover your power and reimagine your purpose again and again. You need pages without lines and limitations to reconnect with your creative, perfectly imperfect self.

Plus, big unlined paper gives you space for more than words. You have plenty of room to doodle, draw or post photographs and clippings, too.

Why color is important?

When you journal, use colored pens and markers! Your world doesn't happen in black and white. Your life should be lived and written about in many colors. Even dark and sad memories feel lighter and brighter when told in color.

Journaling in color affects your mood and perception of your world. Colors evoke calm, cheer and comfort. Using color can lift your spirit and inspire your imagination. You may be surprised by all the beautiful benefits from adding more color into your life story.

When journaling, give yourself time to listen to your heart and reflect. Breathe in the moments. Feel. Be quiet. Let yourself be totally and thoroughly present with your thoughts. Let your heart transform you and teach you new insights. Open your mind to consider new ideas and possibilities. You may find that what your heart teaches will be life changing.

www.ingramcontent.com/pod-product-compliance
Lightning Source LLC
Chambersburg PA
CBHW051252110526
44588CB00025B/2968